THE STORM

A PICTORIAL RECORD OF THE HIGH TIDE OF FEBRUARY 1st 2002 ON THE ISLE OF MAN

COMPILED BY CAPT. ROGER MOORE

All proceeds from this publication

will be donated to the RNLI.

First published 2009

Copyright © 2009 Roger Moore. All rights reserved.

The moral right of the author has been asserted

Published by: Lily Publications Independent

Typeset in Garamond and Solex

ISBN 978-1899602-59-9

CONTENTS

Foreword

The idea for this book started life about six months after the event, when I was reading a local newspaper, which included a photograph of floods which occurred during a very high tide of many years ago. Recalling the press pictures of February 1st 2002, and the remark, much quoted at the time, that it was the 'highest tide in living memory', I wondered if enough photographs had been taken that day, both press and private, to provide sufficient material for a book.

I spoke to John Qualtrough of Cronk Road Port St. Mary, knowing of his work at the Isle of Man College and producing booklets to go with his courses, and a variety of other Manx subjects. He suggested going on Manx Radio to publicise the project, and see if there was any interest. I had an interview with Anne Dawson in October 2002 which was broadcast twice, asking for people to send me any photographs they had taken of that particular high tide. Then it was a question of waiting. No photos, no book!

I was surprised at how good a response we got. Scores of pictures arrived and, while John scanned and filed them, I went round the Island interviewing those people who had provided the photos or whose experiences could add to the story of that day. After an initial burst of enthusiasm, the project lay dormant for a variety of reasons, but hopefully the passage of time has not lessened the impact of some of these remarkable photographs. So here it is. Laa yn sterryn, the day of the storm.

Roger Moore
Port St Mary

Acknowledgements

The first word must go to the people who provided the photographs for this book.

My sincere apologies go to those whose photos I have used but without attribution. Many of these were received as attachments to emails and my attempts to identify them have failed, but heartfelt thanks go to all who most generously allowed me to use their pictures of the storm. There must have been a few wet cameras judging by some of the shots.

I would like to record my great appreciation for the assistance I received from the harbour masters in the various ports in allowing me access to their log books, and of their memories of that day. Also to many other staff from Isle of Man Harbours who gave willingly of their time. In particular to Marion Keelan who was working in the Ramsey harbour office at the time, and whose emails and enthusiasm helped the project along.

Also to the men of the Isle of Man Fire Service, whose memories of this storm and description of the events have added a great deal to the context of the photographs. Many amusing anecdotes were told during my interviews with the firemen, only some of which I have felt able to include!

Grateful thanks also to John K Qualtrough, who scanned hundreds of pictures for me and did much other computer work which helped to move the project forward.

My thanks also go to Dollin Kelly and Paul Reeve who read the proofs and made many useful suggestions, and to my wife Michele for telling me when my writing was getting too 'seafaring'.

Finally, to my friends who have encouraged me over the last few years with comments such as 'When's the book coming out then?', a big thank you for your patience.

Introduction

The high water due at Friday lunchtime on the 1st February 2002 gave little cause for concern in the week leading up to it. True, it was quite a big spring tide, but not an exceptionally high one. In that year alone there were 28 tides expected to be as high or higher, and in the previous five years there had been 139 tides predicted to reach at least the same sea level. However, prolonged, strong southwesterly winds and low atmospheric pressure had combined to cause a severe 'storm surge', an explanation of which, by professional meteorologist Brian Rae, is included as an Appendix. In fact, the combination of meteorological factors on that day were sufficiently unusual for the Proudman Oceanographic Laboratory, working at the Bidston Observatory in Birkenhead, to write a report on the mechanics of this tidal surge and its effect on the whole North Irish Sea area. In this report it states that the sea level in Dublin reached its highest ever recording: a foot higher than the previous record in 1924. On the Isle of Man harbours, promenades, coastal roads, footpaths and properties were flooded, and considerable damage was done over a period of two to three hours.

Small island communities tend to take a greater than usual interest in their weather and the sea, and when this tide was described as being 'the highest in living memory', I thought it would be worthwhile having a good photographic record of the event. Given its location, the Isle of Man is liable to catch the worst that wind and wave can throw at it and it is quite possible that another tide as high, or even higher than this one may well occur in the next decade or so. It is simply a question of all the various factors coming together at the same time. Indeed, as Brian Rae points out in the conclusion to his piece on storm surges, this tide could have been even higher than it was, if the

Introduction...

centre of the depression had passed closer to the Island.

With the expressions 'climate change' and 'global warming' being used these days, seemingly whenever a severe weather event occurs, I was aware that the subject of this storm could take on more significance than it would have done even as little as 20 years ago. Over the past century the mean sea level has been rising at about 2 millimetres per year, and in the last decade or so, the increase has been nearer to 3 millimetres. However, the Proudman Laboratory at Bidston, which operates the Permanent Service for Mean Sea Level, comments '...it is too soon to tell if this is a temporary fluctuation or a long-term change.'

There is a photograph of Albert Street, Ramsey taken about 100 years ago that shows a water level at least as high as during this storm, so perhaps it is best to leave it to the scientists to draw any long-term conclusions.

What I have tried to do in this book, is simply to compile some of the best images of the high tide of the 1st February 2002, and where possible, add comments from interviews with harbour masters, firemen, and some of the photographers themselves, to give context to the pictures. I hope that the result will serve to some degree as a social document, a snapshot, a moment in time, showing the people of the Isle of Man dealing with the exceptional weather conditions in their characteristic and understated way. The traditional Manx way of 'goll as gaccan', roughly translated as 'going and grumbling'.

Roger Moore
Port St. Mary

Douglas

The harbour at Douglas is well sheltered from the southwest but the bay in general, and the north bay around the Derby Castle and Port Jack in particular, are very exposed to heavy seas from this quarter. The wind recorded at the end of the Victoria Pier at 0445 was southerly 42 knots gusting to 58 knots, roughly equivalent to 48 to 67 miles per hour. With the storm surge driving up the Irish Sea, the sea level was running at about 1.4 metres above prediction, quite sufficient to cause flooding problems without the added pressure of the gale. All harbour staff were put on stand-by from half tide onwards.

The commercial traffic in Douglas was quite unusual, due to the fact that the 'Ben my Chree' was in Birkenhead for its biennial overhaul. The 'Lady of Mann' was covering the passenger traffic, while two vessels had been chartered to handle the freight. The 'European

Coffee Palace Berth North Quay.
(*Dr Ruth Nichols*)

Mariner' was berthed at the North Edward Pier, while the 'Belard' and the 'Lady of Mann' were on the South Victoria Pier. The two scheduled sailings for that morning, were the 'Lady' to Liverpool at 0730, and the 'Belard' to Heysham at 0800. Due to the severity of the weather, the Liverpool sailing was delayed until the afternoon, while the freight sailing was cancelled. The 'Lady of Mann' departed for Liverpool at 1600, her log recording a southsouthwest gale for most of the crossing, which took her five hours, and she did not return to the Island until late the next morning. In Birkenhead, the 'Ben my Chree' was lying in dry dock where Captain Ken Crellin was the Master on duty; he observed that the height of this tide in the Mersey had pushed the water level in the dock system to such a height that it was lapping over the dry dock gates.

Now, back to Douglas: the Harbour Master on duty was Nigel Burden, and his telephone must have been red hot with a deluge of calls about broken moorings, boats adrift, smoke coming from electrical boxes, cars and small craft afloat on the Tongue, the North Quay closed due to flooding, and a call from Castletown to report that part of the breakwater wall had fallen away.

The Douglas Fire Service had five vehicles called out, three of which were in the North Quay area where there was extensive flooding. Many of the properties along the quay have cellars but, until the tide started to recede, there was little to be done except make sure no one got into difficulties as the quay edge and other hazards were invisible being underwater. The pumping out could only commence after the tide had started to ebb. There was one fire engine in the Central Promenade area near Broadway where the Empress Hotel suffered damage. The semi-basement restaurant, down a set of steps from the promenade, was taking waves with such force that some large windows were broken.

The other vehicle from the fire station was at the Derby Castle end of the promenade where heavy seas were sweeping across the road, as shown in one of the photographs. Here, cars were floating around and causing damage and the firemen were trying to bring some order to this scene of chaos. All things considered, apart from a lot of drying out, the damage to property in Douglas could have been much worse.

Market Hill is the centre of attention for onlookers and photographers, as the tide creeps up. (*Dr Ruth Nichols*)

Tower of Refuge. (*Dr Ruth Nichols*)

Dr Ruth Nicholls, a member of the Southern and Western Photographic Societies, heard about the high tide on Manx Radio, and set off down to the North Quay. Armed with camera and wellington boots, she took a series of excellent photos.
(*Dr Ruth Nichols*)

A fire crew at the Douglas Hotel.
(*Fenella Carter*)

Not much trade.

Chaos at the Tongue.
(*Dr Ruth Nichols*)

The British Hotel. (*Dr Ruth Nichols*)

Harbour Board divers sort out the
traffic at the Tongue.

Deep water at Leigh Terrace. The
traffic is having to avoid several
wheelie bins which can be seen lying
in the roadway. (*Dr Ruth Nichols*)

Lady of Mann and Belard stormbound
on the South Victoria Pier.
(*Kevin Murphy*)

Outside Clarence Terrace at the
bottom of Broadway. Are these cars
parked or just abandoned?
(*Bill Weldon*)

A police car patrolling the promenade. (*Press picture*)

Waves roll over the road outside the Terminus Tavern. (*Press picture*)

Another great picture at the bottom of
Summer Hill. (*Press picture*)

Laxey

In the normal course of events, the tide starts to flow into Rowe's Dock about three hours before high water. This day, however, there was already a metre of water in the dock at this time, and the signs were there that this was going to be a very big tide. As shown in some of the photographs, the waves roll right over the breakwater in Laxey and up the back of the pier. As the promenade and harbour roads started to flood, an electrical fire started in the Beach Café and the Laxey Fire Service were called to attend to it.

On duty at the harbour was John Cowley, and at 1300, with still an hour to go to high water, he decided to abandon the harbour office due to its exposed position. He spent the next two hours at the upper boat park helping to secure some small craft which were in danger of being washed away. One boat was swept off the park and into the river, where it was quickly taken

Laxey Promenade. (*Brian Quirk*)

Huge waves roll over the breakwater.
John Cowley's car is left to it's fate.
(*Dr Griff Evans*)

out to sea. The remains of this boat were later washed up on Laxey beach. By now John realised it was not possible to retrieve his car, which was parked on the pier by the office, as there was too much water coming over the access road.

At about 1500, when it looked as if the worst was over, John went home to change into dry clothing, and returned to the harbour office to write up the log. Shortly afterwards, at about 1615, there was a bit of a rumbling sound and a gust of wind took the flat roof completely off the building. It fell down the side of the office and lodged against the door, trapping John inside. Luckily, the firemen who had been dealing with the fire in the café, and had then been busy pumping out the pipe factory across the road saw the problem, and hauled the roof away from the office door. John emerged unscathed from what had been quite an exciting afternoon.

It was a month before the office was ready for use again, and John's car was none the worse for its soaking in salt water.

Firemen attend the electrical fire at the Beach Café. During this job, waves were sweeping across the road and into the building, and one fireman was washed off his feet. They were later called to pump out the pipe factory, and finally released John Cowley from the harbour office after the roof blew off. Dr Evans had moved to Laxey in September 2001, and rented a house in Tent Road. The idyllic harbourside location made a favourable impression. This particular Friday he arrived home for lunch to find water entering his front door, with still an hour to go to high water. After moving some possessions to safety in the house, he took his second best camera (due to the amount of spray flying around), and took these dramatic shots'. (*Dr Griff Evans*)

The water cascades into Rowe's Dock amongst the pleasure craft.
(*Brian Quirk*)

Another view of Rowe's Dock, this time from between the boats. The Quirk's holiday cottages can be seen in the background. (*John Cowley*)

Laxey breakwater.
(*Dr Griff Evans*)

A pleasure boat in danger of being
swept into the Laxey River.
(*Brian Quirk*)

The boat is being secured. John
Cowley is in the yellow waterproof
jacket. (*Brian Quirk*)

Looking seaward down Tent Road.
(*Amanda Michel*)

View up Army Hill towards the Noah's
Ark Playschool. (*Tony Jones*)

The Highway Board staff keep an eye on things. (*Amanda Michel*)

After her daughter had been picked up from the Noah's Ark playschool on Army Hill, Amanda Michel returned to Lower Laxey, and took these excellent pictures.

Are the vans safe? (*Amanda Michel*)

Amanda Michel took this picture from
the Zig Zag path at 2pm.
(*Amanda Michel*)

The Harbour Office drying out the next
day. Note the missing roof.
(*Jill Rushton*)

Ramsey

Ramsey Harbour is well sheltered from the south west, so the strong winds and heavy seas of this storm were not likely to cause structural damage as happened in the south and east of the Island. In fact, Ramsey Bay is one of the best places in the Irish Sea for a ship to find shelter in conditions like this. The problem for Ramsey, as it has always been, is flooding. The quay area, Market Place, Parliament Street and as far back as Albert Road are all low-lying, and Riverside above the Bowring Road bridge is also vulnerable.

The Harbour Log at 0700 recorded a barometric pressure of 1010 millibars, with a sustained wind speed of 40 knots, gusting to 66 knots from the south-southwest.

On duty at the harbour that morning was Martin

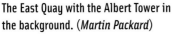

The East Quay with the Albert Tower in the background. (*Martin Packard*)

Looking seaward on West Quay.
(*Mike Bolton*)

Packard assisted by Paul Hay.

The East Quay was busy, with the 'Auldyn River' and the 'Ben Ellan' arriving just before midnight, to join the 'Ben Maye', which was already in port. As there is only room for two coasters alongside the East Quay, the 'Ben Ellan' moored alongside the 'Ben Maye'.

At 1100 the 'Ben Ellan' sailed to anchor in the bay, to allow the 'Ben Maye' and 'Auldyn River' to swap places on the East Quay to allow access to cranes. This was the position over the high water period and in the photographs shown in this chapter. While cargo work was suspended over the worst of the flooding, commercial operations in Ramsey Harbour were very little affected by the storm and this exceptional tide.

Most of the private boat owners, being aware of the weather, were down attending to their craft. At 1230, the harbour log recorded the quay, town and boat park started flooding, with still over an hour to go to high water.

The Ramsey Fire Service was called out shortly after 1300 to deal with the flooding and any other emergencies that might arise while access to the lower town was affected. The pagers going off came as no

The Peel registered fishing vessels 'Venture Again' and 'Sincerity' double banked opposite the Trafalgar Hotel. (*Mike Bolton*)

surprise to the fire crews as they were well aware of the strong winds overnight and the expected high tide. However, they were not expecting the extra four feet of water added by the storm surge which came as a surprise to everyone. All three appliances were out around the town dealing with situations as they arose, and distributing sand bags to the most vulnerable properties and businesses. There were road works in Parliament Street which presented an added problem. This involved a trench down the centre of the street, three feet deep in places but partly filled in and marked with cones. As the street filled with water the cones started to move around leaving the now invisible trench unmarked. As the firemen had plenty of work to do in the street, this hazard came into play, and there were reports of the occasional accidental visit to the 'hole in the road'!

As the tide started to recede, many properties, cellars and basements had to be pumped out, some of them for the second time. The firemen finally returned to base at 2200, nine hours after the first call out.

Ben Maye and fire engine on East
Quay. (*Martin Packard*)

Cargo work is suspended on the East
Quay. (*Mike Bolton*)

View over harbour towards Mooragh
Park. (*Mike Bolton*)

Waders are the fashion on the East
Quay. (*Martin Packard*)

On a day like this, it's a good idea to
put a mooring rope on your car.
(*Martin Packard*)

The swing bridge at high water.
(*Norman Leece*)

As the tide recedes, the firemen start pumping out a cellar. Fishing vessel 'Frey' and 'Ben Maye' in the foreground. (*Norman Leece*)

The crew of the 'Auldyn River' have just put out a new mooring rope after the backspring has parted. All under the watchful eye of their Managing Director, who took the picture. (*Norman Leece*)

St Paul's Church. (*Mike Bolton*)

Albert Sreet with Quayle's Hall on the
right. This is two streets back from
the quay! (*Mike Bolton*)

Electricity and water don't mix. The switch box in Market Place.
(*Martin Packard*)

Parliament Street looking south east.
(*Mike Bolton*)

Parliament Street looking north west.
Mind the hole! (*Keith Swales*)

Firemen at work in Parliament Street.
(*Keith Swales*)

Selling houses. Business as usual.
(*Keith Swales*)

Riverside Lane. (*Martin Packard*)

Ben Ellan anchored in the bay.
(*Martin Packard*)

Ramsey promenade. (*Norman Leece*)

Peel

The north and west coast of the Island emerged relatively unscathed from this storm and, as the photographs from Peel show, there was only slight flooding around the harbour areas.

Michael Cannan was on harbour duty and the log simply recorded the exceptionally high tide, the wind during the morning as southsouthwest gale force 8, and that no damage was caused around the harbour.

The Quay by the Peel Heritage Museum. (*Roy Baker*)

East Quay looking towards the castle.
(*Roy Baker*)

Four Peel lads on the way home with
wet feet. (*Roy Baker*)

View up the River Neb towards the
West Marine workshops.
(*Pauline Oliver*)

The Creek Inn has some mopping up
to do. (*Pauline Oliver*)

Two photos from Brian Maddrell of his boat 'Fulmar' lying on the West Quay. Even though she is well fendered, he is keeping a close eye on her to make sure she does not ride up over the quay. In the first picture, the new chimney of the Power Station is in the background. In the second picture, the Harbour Office and 'Spit Corner' are in the background. (*Brian Maddrell*)

There could be more fenders required
at the East Quay. (*Pauline Oliver*)

Fishing Vessels lie at Peel Breakwater
untroubled by the storm or the height
of the tide. From left to right, 'La
Belle Trois', 'Silver Viking', 'Vervine',
and the 'Zephyr'. (*Brian Maddrell*)

Traffic passing the House of Manannan.
(*Pauline Oliver*)

Another photo from Brian Maddrell looking seaward. (*Brian Maddrell*)

Port Erin

It is only one mile across the neck of land from Port Erin to Port St. Mary but the contrast in sea conditions can often be extreme. On this occasion, while Port St. Mary was being battered by the storm, Port Erin was a peaceful harbour with no signs of the drama that was going on elsewhere. Only one contributor, Dick Leece, thought it worthwhile to take a photo of Port Erin as well as Port St. Mary over this tide.

The comparative calm in Port Erin could have been the reason the Port Erin fire crew thought the run to Castletown would be fairly straightforward. Their first call out was at 1315 to attend an electrical fire at Qualtrough's Timber Yard. The Castletown fire engines were already busy handling several other incidents in the town.

Unaware of the severity of this storm, the Port Erin

All looks quiet in Port Erin.
(*Dick Leece*)

appliance headed for the Shore Road route to Castletown, arriving at the old Shore Garage junction at the very top of this high tide.

The fire engine could probably have made it safely along the road with that depth of water, but many large stones were in the roadway, thrown over the sea wall by the waves. This posed a significant risk of damage to the vehicle, so the decision was made to take a diversion. These moments were captured in the dramatic photos on pages 56 and 57 taken by Mark Wilson as the Port Erin fire engine, up to it's axles and covered in spray, turned off the Shore Road, up Mount Gawne Road, and on to Castletown via Colby. On arriving at the timber yard, there was more excitement when the Station Officer (now retired), stepped out into flood water deeper than expected, and got his boots full of water: something he has not been allowed to forget. Photos of the Port Erin fire crew working at the timber yard are in the Castletown chapter.

The smaller fire tender from Port Erin was also called to Castletown, to attend to the flooding at the Canada Life office building at Alexandra Bridge. The story and photos of this are also in the Castletown chapter.

The lower promenade remained dry right over the high tide.
(*Dick Leece*)

Port St. Mary

At the time of this storm the new harbour office at the root of the Alfred Pier had just been completed and was in use, but the weather recording equipment was not fully operational. Only the barometer readings were available. The building was officially opened three months later on April 29th 2002.

On duty on this memorable day were Chris Burton and Alan Preston. The weather was recorded in the morning as a southsouthwesterly gale with a heavy sea and swell, and a barometer reading of 989 millibars.

The following is a summary of the entries in the harbour log.

'Heavy seas on breakwater causing extensive damage to Mariners' Shelter, fish factory, tin huts, wood huts, waste oil tank and lifeboat oil storage area.

Inner Harbour.
(*Stan Sille*)

Kallow Point.
(*Stan Sille*)

Heavy flooding in Lime Street and boat park. Hole in surface of boat park and at top of slipway. One Orkney Class boat missing from boat park, owner informed. (This boat was subsequently found to have been blown with its trailer off the park, into the sea, and swept two miles across Bay ny Carrickey and wrecked on the shore at Poyll Vaaish). Two boats stored on beach at inner harbour possibly damaged. Section of back wall of breakwater damaged. Alfred Pier lighting section shorted out. Wash boards broken and numerous covers and concrete areas damaged'.

The Mariners' Shelter was so badly damaged that it had to be demolished, and was rebuilt beside the lifeboat slipway as part of a new pump house.

It was reopened on June 26th 2005 by Peter Quirk jnr. The original shelter had been opened in 1987 in memory of his father, Peter Quirk, better known as 'Kettle', a fisherman, local politician and larger than life character, whose untimely death in 1986 left the Port and the wider fishing community very much the poorer.

The breakwater lighthouse survived another seven years, before being completely swept off the end of the pier in a fairly standard winter gale on the night of Sunday 11th January 2009.

The fishing boats are dancing at the
Alfred Pier. 'De Bounty' 'Fenella Ann'
'Maureen Patricia' 'Friendly Shore'
and the Lifeboat 'Gough Ritchie 2'.
(*Stan Sille*)

Another excellent photo from Stan
Sille, showing the boats hanging on
at the full stretch of their moorings.
(*Stan Sille*)

The back of Alfred Pier about two
hours after high water showing
damage to the fish factory.
(*Alex Maddrell*)

Flooded boat park with old kipper
house in foreground. (*Alex Maddrell*)

Some of the damage to the surface of
the boat park. Note Alex Maddrell's
weather proof camera case.
(*Alex Maddrell*)

Flood water behind Lime Street.
IOM Yacht Club building in the
background. (*Alex Maddrell*)

The dinghys normally kept on the
slipway have been hauled down Lime
Street for safety. (*Dick Leece*)

More photos being taken at the inner
harbour slipway. (*Dick Clague*)

The inner harbour looking towards
Lime Street. The hand rails on
Boolavur jetty are just visible.
(*John W Qualtrough*)

The Isle of Man Harbours workboat
'Tarroo Ushtey' lies at the seaward
end of the Inner Harbour.
(*John W Qualtrough*)

The Underway. From the Chicken Rock
Lighthouse store in the foreground,
round Chapel Bay to Gansey Point and
on out to Kentraugh, suffered the
worst of the damage in this storm.
(*John W Qualtrough*)

Taken below the Carrick Bay
Apartments, this shows the start of
the catwalk, most of which was
destroyed. Gansey Point in the
background. (*Stan Sille*)

Catwalk. (*John W Qualtrough*)

Lower Promenade.
(*John W Qualtrough*)

This and the two previous pictures by
John Qualtrough show the damage
being sustained by the catwalk, the
sea wall, and the retaining wall to the
brooghs at Chapel Bay.
(*John W Qualtrough*)

Gansey Point. (*Margaret Brierley*)

The slipway at Gansey Point, with the
Inner Harbour and the Carrick Bay
Apartments in the background.
(*Eric Alexander*)

Garden furniture is being washed up
Beach Road. Several houses along this
stretch had their garden walls
knocked down. (*Roger Moore*)

This footpath leads past the Studio, and around Gansey Point to Chapel Bay. (*Roger Moore*)

Beach Road looking east towards the Shore Hotel and Kentraugh. The road was underwater to this depth for two hours, as the drains failed to cope with the amount of water coming over the sea wall. (*Roger Moore*)

Damage to the underway below the
Carrick Bay Apartments. (*Stan Sille*)

This property on Beach Road has lost
part of its garden wall. (*Mark Wilson*)

The Port Erin fire engine en route to Castletown passing the old Shore Garage. The Shore Hotel and Kentraugh Hill are in the background. (*Mark Wilson*)

The reversing lights are on, as they encounter large stones in the road. (*Mark Wilson*)

After leaving Qualtrough's Timber Yard, this vehicle was called to the Shore Hotel at the bottom of Kentraugh Hill, which can be seen in the background of the photo on the opposite page. The pub had suffered damage when the sea and stones had smashed the doors to the beer cellar and flooded it out. The licensee had only just taken over at the 'Shore' a few months earlier, and was engaged in a major refurbishment, which meant that a lot of new equipment was in the beer cellar waiting to be fitted. Many thousands of pounds worth of fittings were ruined by the salt water. Then a skip, containing about a ton of stone for the building work, floated off into the car park behind the pub driven by the force of the heavy seas. The licensee, Debbie Lagden, had her leg in plaster from an accident a few weeks earlier so, altogether, it was not a good day for this lady. However, with her typical Yorkshire determination, the refurbishment was completed, and she is still in charge at the Shore Hotel today.

To get to the pub, the fire engine had to drive down the Croit y Caley road from the Colby Level, which runs beside the Colby River. The high tide had backed up the river, which had flooded over the road, allowing the

The fire engine heads off up Mount Gawne Road, and so to Castletown via Colby. (*Mark Wilson*)

resident ducks to swim around in front of the vehicle. Unfortunately, no pictures! There were still a lot of waves coming over the road in front of the Shore Hotel so the fire engine was parked to form a shelter of sorts for the crew while they pumped out the cellar.

After this, there were various calls to domestic property around Port St Mary, especially Lime Street and the Underway. Sandbags were handed out too, in case they were needed for the next high tide due at two o'clock the next morning. The crews were finally stood down and, after returning to base and cleaning up, it was not far short of midnight.

The following day. What's left of the catwalk. (*Stan Sille*)

Castletown

Castletown Bay faces south west, straight into the teeth of this gale, so the breakwater and sea defences were going to be severely tested. The officer on duty at Castletown this Friday was Tony Sloan, and the harbour log recorded a wind speed of 33-36 knots from the southwest at 0830 in the morning. At 1230, with over an hour to go to high water, Tony went to the upper harbour to check on the boat park, as the water was starting to flood over the West Quay. To get there dry shod he had to walk down Hope Street, where there was already a foot of water in places. Properties in this area were being protected with sand bags. On returning to the harbour office just after one o'clock, it was clear that the breakwater was taking a terrific pounding and, at about half past one, a section of the upper wall started to collapse. Surprisingly, the damage

Breakwater.
(*John Cole*)

did not spread and was confined to the landward end of the wall.

The first call out for the Castletown Fire Service was to the properties at the corner of Douglas Street, (The Rock and Bridge House), which were taking a lot of water over their walls. This was partly due to the height of the tide, but mostly the result of the very heavy seas coming in over the rocks. Further along Douglas Street, the road was awash and many properties had water up to their front doors. The promenade out towards Hango Hill had a lot of water coming over but the sea defences along here stood up well. The fire crews were also called to the Castle Arms Hotel, (The Glue Pot) where they had water in the cellars. As the sea level just kept on rising, the water flowed over Victoria Road and into the properties close to Alexandra Bridge. The photographs of the fire engines in this chapter show them shuttling between the various jobs. It was at this stage that Qualtrough's Timber Yard reported an electrical fire, and the Canada Life office building at Alexandra Bridge started to flood. With the Castletown appliances fully occupied, the Port Erin Brigade were called in to assist, the pictures of their exciting journey appearing in the Port St Mary chapter. The Castletown firemen were finally stood down at 9pm so there may have just been time for a pint.

Castletown breakwater suffered a fearful battering in this storm, but apart from losing part of the upper wall, it stood up remarkably well. (*John Cole*)

The Chairman of Castletown Commissioners, John Cringle checks up on his boat. This superb photo by John Cole gives some idea of the size and power of the waves generated by this storm. (*John Cole*)

Where did all this water come from? (*Ship Inn Photography Group*)

Taking shelter. This cormorant took up residence in the dinghy, and stayed for three days. (*Kath Cooil*)

The larger Castletown fire engine carefully navigates its way up Victoria Road making the minimum of bow wave. (*Ship Inn Photography Group*)

The Port Erin fire engine arriving at the timber yard, after their adventurous journey from the fire station. (*Ship Inn Photography Group*)

Discussing tactics.

At the lower end of Hope Street, residents take things like this in their stride. (*Kath Cooil*)

Back Hope Street. The tide is level with the West Quay.

Photo bottom left
(*Kath Cooil*)
Photo bottom right
(*Ship Inn Photography Group*)

The harbour entrance to the Ship Inn is flooded... But lunchtime drinkers make their escape out the back door into Hope Street. (*Kath Cooil*)

What a day. (*Kath Cooil*)

Flooding on the Umber Quay.
(*Kath Cooil*)

The bucket line at Canada Life Office,
Alexandra Bridge. (*Phil Kneen*)

Appendix 1
1st February 2002
A Meteorological Perspective

The rhythmic rise and fall of the world's oceans, and the times and heights of high and low water at any particular location depend for the most part on the relative positions of the Earth, Moon and Sun. The Earth and the Moon orbit with a regularity that makes it possible to make tidal predictions years in advance which are accurate enough for most practical purposes. When the Moon and the Sun line up with the Earth each month, the combined gravitational attraction produces the highest or 'spring tides'. Conversely, when the Earth is at right angles to a line through the Moon and the Sun we have smaller or 'neap' tides.

That is not the whole story, because the tide tables produced from astronomical predictions ignore the variable effects of the atmosphere on our oceans. Higher than average atmospheric pressure will depress the sea level. Very low pressure can allow the sea surface to well up to a level, which is significantly higher than predicted. Strong winds will also move water from one part of an ocean to another, and these surges on the sea surface can make a further addition to the height of the tide. Finally, if the fetch is right, or in other words, if a strong wind blows for a long time over a long stretch of water it will build up a swell and very heavy seas.

These scenarios are not uncommon in themselves. Spring tides are a monthly event and low pressure and gales are fairly common at mid latitudes, especially during winter. However, on the rare occasions when a very big spring tide coincides with an exceptionally

Photo courtesy of Dundee University

deep low and very strong winds, it can cause serious problems in coastal areas.

The weather during the last few days of January 2002 was fairly typical of that time of year with low pressure over much of the North Atlantic. Strong or gale force southwest winds were driving seas towards the British Isles with a long, straight fetch that originated near to the Azores. Indeed, it was to the north of the Azores on the last day of the month that a low which already had a central pressure of 978 millibars was showing signs of deepening rapidly as it transferred northeastward. During Friday morning, 1st February, that low passed about 500 nautical miles to the northwest of the Isle of Man. By then though, the centre was down to about 932 millibars and so despite the fact that it was so far distant, it produced a severe gale force southsouthwesterly in the Irish Sea for a time, just ahead of a cold front. Mean speeds at Ronaldsway were close to 50mph with a maximum gust of 68mph. The gales had abated by the time of high tide in the early afternoon but the damage had been done. The severe gales and the very big fall in pressure in the near Atlantic had produced a very big sea and a 'storm surge' which added a metre or more to a big spring tide.

One cannot help wondering what might have happened if the centre of the low had passed closer to the Isle of Man or if the gale had continued through the time of high water.
— *Brian Rae*

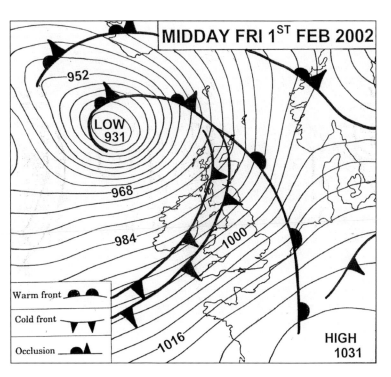

Ths chart shows the exceptional depth of the low which drove so much water into the Irish Sea.

Appendix 2

The breakwater at Port St. Mary, properly referred to as the Alfred Pier, was completed in 1886. The 'pepper pot' lighthouse at the end, is said to have come from the Port Erin breakwater which was destroyed by storms in 1884.

It stood up to all weathers for over 120 years without significant damage.

However, just before midnight on Sunday 11th January 2009, it was swept completely off the pier; this left only the six bed bolts and a bit of debris stuck to the railings, in what was otherwise an unremarkable winter gale.

The lifebuoy which was mounted on the lighthouse was later found on Gansey Point, half a mile away.

These three pictures were taken
on the 12th January, about 12
hours after the incident.

These pictures were taken on the 10th March.

Taken 22nd March.